Beating the Casinos at Gambling
for Geniuses

By Wanda Bet

www.justforgeniuses.com

DISCLAIMER: The book is a work of parody. Nothing in this book is meant to imply any facts about any actual persons or entities.

All rights reserved. No part of this publication may be reproduced, distributed, or transmitted in any form or by any means, including photocopying, recording, or other electronic or mechanical methods, without the prior written permission of the publisher.

Copyright © 2014 by Westlake Gavin Publishers LLC

Just for Geniuses, For Geniuses, and accompanying logos are trademarks of Westlake Gavin Publishers LLC and may not be used without written permission. All other trademarks are the property of their respective owners. Westlake Gavin Publishers LLC, is not associated with any other product or service mentioned in this book.

HUMANS OF MIRTH COLLECTION   TGGT1003

Library of *Con*-gress Cataloging-in-Publication Data

Beating the Casinos at Gambling for Geniuses / by Wanda Bet
p. cm.
ISBN 978-1-63231-996-8
1. Bet, Wanda 2. Parody, imitations, etc. I. Title.

First Edition

10 9 8 7 6 5 4 3 2 1

Inside...

The secrets that casinos don't want you to know.

Make more money than you've every made gambling before. Easy to learn. No counting cards. No complicated rules.

No traveling required. Works in the privacy of your own home.

Works effectively with any amount of capital. No amount is too large or too small.

Say goodbye to losing streaks. From now on, you win all the time, every time.

Best part: casinos will never, ever see another dime of your money.

And so much more...

Beating the Casinos at Gambling *for Geniuses*

Flush your money down the toilet.

Yes, that's how easy and fun it is. Let me explain. Over time, both flushing your money down the toilet and gambling will be equally effective at making your money vanish. But since it takes less time to flush your money down the toilet than to gamble it away—and time is money—flushing your money down the toilet is hands-down the winning strategy.

Beating the Casinos at Gambling *for Geniuses*

Flush your money down the toilet.

Yes, that's how easy and fun it is. Let me explain. Over time, both flushing your money down the toilet and gambling will be equally effective at making your money vanish. But since it takes less time to flush your money down the toilet than to gamble it away—and time is money—flushing your money down the toilet is hands-down the winning strategy.

Read enough? Turn to page 104

Flush your money down the toilet.

Yes, that's how easy and fun it is. Let me explain. Over time, both flushing your money down the toilet and gambling will be equally effective at making your money vanish. But since it takes less time to flush your money down the toilet than to gamble it away—and time is money—flushing your money down the toilet is hands-down the winning strategy.

Read enough? Turn to page 104

Flush your money down the toilet.

Yes, that's how easy and fun it is. Let me explain. Over time, both flushing your money down the toilet and gambling will be equally effective at making your money vanish. But since it takes less time to flush your money down the toilet than to gamble it away—and time is money—flushing your money down the toilet is hands-down the winning strategy.

Read enough? Turn to page 104

Beating the Casinos at Gambling *for Geniuses*

Flush your money down the toilet.

Yes, that's how easy and fun it is. Let me explain. Over time, both flushing your money down the toilet and gambling will be equally effective at making your money vanish. But since it takes less time to flush your money down the toilet than to gamble it away—and time is money—flushing your money down the toilet is hands-down the winning strategy.

Read enough? Turn to page 104

Flush your money down the toilet.

Yes, that's how easy and fun it is. Let me explain. Over time, both flushing your money down the toilet and gambling will be equally effective at making your money vanish. But since it takes less time to flush your money down the toilet than to gamble it away—and time is money—flushing your money down the toilet is hands-down the winning strategy.

Read enough? Turn to page 104

Beating the Casinos at Gambling *for Geniuses*

Flush your money down the toilet.

Yes, that's how easy and fun it is. Let me explain. Over time, both flushing your money down the toilet and gambling will be equally effective at making your money vanish. But since it takes less time to flush your money down the toilet than to gamble it away—and time is money—flushing your money down the toilet is hands-down the winning strategy.

Read enough? Turn to page 104

Flush your money down the toilet.

Yes, that's how easy and fun it is. Let me explain. Over time, both flushing your money down the toilet and gambling will be equally effective at making your money vanish. But since it takes less time to flush your money down the toilet than to gamble it away—and time is money—flushing your money down the toilet is hands-down the winning strategy.

Read enough? Turn to page 104

Beating the Casinos at Gambling *for Geniuses*

Flush your money down the toilet.

Yes, that's how easy and fun it is. Let me explain. Over time, both flushing your money down the toilet and gambling will be equally effective at making your money vanish. But since it takes less time to flush your money down the toilet than to gamble it away—and time is money—flushing your money down the toilet is hands-down the winning strategy.

Read enough? Turn to page 104

Beating the Casinos at Gambling *for Geniuses*

Flush your money down the toilet.

Yes, that's how easy and fun it is. Let me explain. Over time, both flushing your money down the toilet and gambling will be equally effective at making your money vanish. But since it takes less time to flush your money down the toilet than to gamble it away—and time is money—flushing your money down the toilet is hands-down the winning strategy.

Read enough? Turn to page 104

Flush your money down the toilet.

Yes, that's how easy and fun it is. Let me explain. Over time, both flushing your money down the toilet and gambling will be equally effective at making your money vanish. But since it takes less time to flush your money down the toilet than to gamble it away—and time is money—flushing your money down the toilet is hands-down the winning strategy.

Read enough? Turn to page 104

Flush your money down the toilet.

Yes, that's how easy and fun it is. Let me explain. Over time, both flushing your money down the toilet and gambling will be equally effective at making your money vanish. But since it takes less time to flush your money down the toilet than to gamble it away—and time is money—flushing your money down the toilet is hands-down the winning strategy.

Read enough? Turn to page 104

Flush your money down the toilet.

Yes, that's how easy and fun it is. Let me explain. Over time, both flushing your money down the toilet and gambling will be equally effective at making your money vanish. But since it takes less time to flush your money down the toilet than to gamble it away—and time is money—flushing your money down the toilet is hands-down the winning strategy.

Read enough? Turn to page 104

Beating the Casinos at Gambling *for Geniuses*

Flush your money down the toilet.

Yes, that's how easy and fun it is. Let me explain. Over time, both flushing your money down the toilet and gambling will be equally effective at making your money vanish. But since it takes less time to flush your money down the toilet than to gamble it away—and time is money—flushing your money down the toilet is hands-down the winning strategy.

Read enough? Turn to page 104

Beating the Casinos at Gambling *for Geniuses*

Flush your money down the toilet.

Yes, that's how easy and fun it is. Let me explain. Over time, both flushing your money down the toilet and gambling will be equally effective at making your money vanish. But since it takes less time to flush your money down the toilet than to gamble it away—and time is money—flushing your money down the toilet is hands-down the winning strategy.

Read enough? Turn to page 104

Beating the Casinos at Gambling *for Geniuses*

Flush your money down the toilet.

Yes, that's how easy and fun it is. Let me explain. Over time, both flushing your money down the toilet and gambling will be equally effective at making your money vanish. But since it takes less time to flush your money down the toilet than to gamble it away—and time is money—flushing your money down the toilet is hands-down the winning strategy.

Read enough? Turn to page 104

Beating the Casinos at Gambling *for Geniuses*

Flush your money down the toilet.

Yes, that's how easy and fun it is. Let me explain. Over time, both flushing your money down the toilet and gambling will be equally effective at making your money vanish. But since it takes less time to flush your money down the toilet than to gamble it away—and time is money—flushing your money down the toilet is hands-down the winning strategy.

Read enough? Turn to page 104

Flush your money down the toilet.

Yes, that's how easy and fun it is. Let me explain. Over time, both flushing your money down the toilet and gambling will be equally effective at making your money vanish. But since it takes less time to flush your money down the toilet than to gamble it away—and time is money—flushing your money down the toilet is hands-down the winning strategy.

Read enough? Turn to page 104

Beating the Casinos at Gambling *for Geniuses*

Flush your money down the toilet.

Yes, that's how easy and fun it is. Let me explain. Over time, both flushing your money down the toilet and gambling will be equally effective at making your money vanish. But since it takes less time to flush your money down the toilet than to gamble it away—and time is money—flushing your money down the toilet is hands-down the winning strategy.

Read enough? Turn to page 104

Beating the Casinos at Gambling *for Geniuses*

Flush your money down the toilet.

Yes, that's how easy and fun it is. Let me explain. Over time, both flushing your money down the toilet and gambling will be equally effective at making your money vanish. But since it takes less time to flush your money down the toilet than to gamble it away—and time is money—flushing your money down the toilet is hands-down the winning strategy.

Read enough? Turn to page 104

Flush your money down the toilet.

Yes, that's how easy and fun it is. Let me explain. Over time, both flushing your money down the toilet and gambling will be equally effective at making your money vanish. But since it takes less time to flush your money down the toilet than to gamble it away—and time is money—flushing your money down the toilet is hands-down the winning strategy.

Read enough? Turn to page 104

Flush your money down the toilet.

Yes, that's how easy and fun it is. Let me explain. Over time, both flushing your money down the toilet and gambling will be equally effective at making your money vanish. But since it takes less time to flush your money down the toilet than to gamble it away—and time is money—flushing your money down the toilet is hands-down the winning strategy.

Read enough? Turn to page 104

Flush your money down the toilet.

Yes, that's how easy and fun it is. Let me explain. Over time, both flushing your money down the toilet and gambling will be equally effective at making your money vanish. But since it takes less time to flush your money down the toilet than to gamble it away—and time is money—flushing your money down the toilet is hands-down the winning strategy.

Read enough? Turn to page 104

Flush your money down the toilet.

Yes, that's how easy and fun it is. Let me explain. Over time, both flushing your money down the toilet and gambling will be equally effective at making your money vanish. But since it takes less time to flush your money down the toilet than to gamble it away—and time is money—flushing your money down the toilet is hands-down the winning strategy.

Read enough? Turn to page 104

Flush your money down the toilet.

Yes, that's how easy and fun it is. Let me explain. Over time, both flushing your money down the toilet and gambling will be equally effective at making your money vanish. But since it takes less time to flush your money down the toilet than to gamble it away—and time is money—flushing your money down the toilet is hands-down the winning strategy.

Read enough? Turn to page 104

Beating the Casinos at Gambling *for Geniuses*

Flush your money down the toilet.

Yes, that's how easy and fun it is. Let me explain. Over time, both flushing your money down the toilet and gambling will be equally effective at making your money vanish. But since it takes less time to flush your money down the toilet than to gamble it away—and time is money—flushing your money down the toilet is hands-down the winning strategy.

Read enough? Turn to page 104

Flush your money down the toilet.

Yes, that's how easy and fun it is. Let me explain. Over time, both flushing your money down the toilet and gambling will be equally effective at making your money vanish. But since it takes less time to flush your money down the toilet than to gamble it away—and time is money—flushing your money down the toilet is hands-down the winning strategy.

Read enough? Turn to page 104

Beating the Casinos at Gambling *for Geniuses*

Flush your money down the toilet.

Yes, that's how easy and fun it is. Let me explain. Over time, both flushing your money down the toilet and gambling will be equally effective at making your money vanish. But since it takes less time to flush your money down the toilet than to gamble it away—and time is money—flushing your money down the toilet is hands-down the winning strategy.

Read enough? Turn to page 104

Flush your money down the toilet.

Yes, that's how easy and fun it is. Let me explain. Over time, both flushing your money down the toilet and gambling will be equally effective at making your money vanish. But since it takes less time to flush your money down the toilet than to gamble it away—and time is money—flushing your money down the toilet is hands-down the winning strategy.

Read enough? Turn to page 104

Flush your money down the toilet.

Yes, that's how easy and fun it is. Let me explain. Over time, both flushing your money down the toilet and gambling will be equally effective at making your money vanish. But since it takes less time to flush your money down the toilet than to gamble it away—and time is money—flushing your money down the toilet is hands-down the winning strategy.

Read enough? Turn to page 104

Flush your money down the toilet.

Yes, that's how easy and fun it is. Let me explain. Over time, both flushing your money down the toilet and gambling will be equally effective at making your money vanish. But since it takes less time to flush your money down the toilet than to gamble it away—and time is money—flushing your money down the toilet is hands-down the winning strategy.

Read enough? Turn to page 104

Flush your money down the toilet.

Yes, that's how easy and fun it is. Let me explain. Over time, both flushing your money down the toilet and gambling will be equally effective at making your money vanish. But since it takes less time to flush your money down the toilet than to gamble it away—and time is money—flushing your money down the toilet is hands-down the winning strategy.

Read enough? Turn to page 104

Flush your money down the toilet.

Yes, that's how easy and fun it is. Let me explain. Over time, both flushing your money down the toilet and gambling will be equally effective at making your money vanish. But since it takes less time to flush your money down the toilet than to gamble it away—and time is money—flushing your money down the toilet is hands-down the winning strategy.

Read enough? Turn to page 104

Flush your money down the toilet.

Yes, that's how easy and fun it is. Let me explain. Over time, both flushing your money down the toilet and gambling will be equally effective at making your money vanish. But since it takes less time to flush your money down the toilet than to gamble it away—and time is money—flushing your money down the toilet is hands-down the winning strategy.

Read enough? Turn to page 104

Beating the Casinos at Gambling *for Geniuses*

Flush your money down the toilet.

Yes, that's how easy and fun it is. Let me explain. Over time, both flushing your money down the toilet and gambling will be equally effective at making your money vanish. But since it takes less time to flush your money down the toilet than to gamble it away—and time is money—flushing your money down the toilet is hands-down the winning strategy.

Read enough? Turn to page 104

Beating the Casinos at Gambling *for Geniuses*

Flush your money down the toilet.

Yes, that's how easy and fun it is. Let me explain. Over time, both flushing your money down the toilet and gambling will be equally effective at making your money vanish. But since it takes less time to flush your money down the toilet than to gamble it away—and time is money—flushing your money down the toilet is hands-down the winning strategy.

Read enough? Turn to page 104

Flush your money down the toilet.

Yes, that's how easy and fun it is. Let me explain. Over time, both flushing your money down the toilet and gambling will be equally effective at making your money vanish. But since it takes less time to flush your money down the toilet than to gamble it away—and time is money—flushing your money down the toilet is hands-down the winning strategy.

Read enough? Turn to page 104

Flush your money down the toilet.

Yes, that's how easy and fun it is. Let me explain. Over time, both flushing your money down the toilet and gambling will be equally effective at making your money vanish. But since it takes less time to flush your money down the toilet than to gamble it away—and time is money—flushing your money down the toilet is hands-down the winning strategy.

Read enough? Turn to page 104

Beating the Casinos at Gambling *for Geniuses*

Flush your money down the toilet.

Yes, that's how easy and fun it is. Let me explain. Over time, both flushing your money down the toilet and gambling will be equally effective at making your money vanish. But since it takes less time to flush your money down the toilet than to gamble it away—and time is money—flushing your money down the toilet is hands-down the winning strategy.

Read enough? Turn to page 104

Flush your money down the toilet.

Yes, that's how easy and fun it is. Let me explain. Over time, both flushing your money down the toilet and gambling will be equally effective at making your money vanish. But since it takes less time to flush your money down the toilet than to gamble it away—and time is money—flushing your money down the toilet is hands-down the winning strategy.

Read enough? Turn to page 104

Flush your money down the toilet.

Yes, that's how easy and fun it is. Let me explain. Over time, both flushing your money down the toilet and gambling will be equally effective at making your money vanish. But since it takes less time to flush your money down the toilet than to gamble it away—and time is money—flushing your money down the toilet is hands-down the winning strategy.

Read enough? Turn to page 104

Beating the Casinos at Gambling *for Geniuses*

Flush your money down the toilet.

Yes, that's how easy and fun it is. Let me explain. Over time, both flushing your money down the toilet and gambling will be equally effective at making your money vanish. But since it takes less time to flush your money down the toilet than to gamble it away—and time is money—flushing your money down the toilet is hands-down the winning strategy.

Read enough? Turn to page 104

Flush your money down the toilet.

Yes, that's how easy and fun it is. Let me explain. Over time, both flushing your money down the toilet and gambling will be equally effective at making your money vanish. But since it takes less time to flush your money down the toilet than to gamble it away—and time is money—flushing your money down the toilet is hands-down the winning strategy.

Read enough? Turn to page 104

Beating the Casinos at Gambling *for Geniuses*

Flush your money down the toilet.

Yes, that's how easy and fun it is. Let me explain. Over time, both flushing your money down the toilet and gambling will be equally effective at making your money vanish. But since it takes less time to flush your money down the toilet than to gamble it away—and time is money—flushing your money down the toilet is hands-down the winning strategy.

Read enough? Turn to page 104

Beating the Casinos at Gambling *for Geniuses*

Flush your money down the toilet.

Yes, that's how easy and fun it is. Let me explain. Over time, both flushing your money down the toilet and gambling will be equally effective at making your money vanish. But since it takes less time to flush your money down the toilet than to gamble it away—and time is money—flushing your money down the toilet is hands-down the winning strategy.

Read enough? Turn to page 104

Flush your money down the toilet.

Yes, that's how easy and fun it is. Let me explain. Over time, both flushing your money down the toilet and gambling will be equally effective at making your money vanish. But since it takes less time to flush your money down the toilet than to gamble it away—and time is money—flushing your money down the toilet is hands-down the winning strategy.

Read enough? Turn to page 104

Beating the Casinos at Gambling *for Geniuses*

Flush your money down the toilet.

Yes, that's how easy and fun it is. Let me explain. Over time, both flushing your money down the toilet and gambling will be equally effective at making your money vanish. But since it takes less time to flush your money down the toilet than to gamble it away—and time is money—flushing your money down the toilet is hands-down the winning strategy.

Read enough? Turn to page 104

Flush your money down the toilet.

Yes, that's how easy and fun it is. Let me explain. Over time, both flushing your money down the toilet and gambling will be equally effective at making your money vanish. But since it takes less time to flush your money down the toilet than to gamble it away—and time is money—flushing your money down the toilet is hands-down the winning strategy.

Read enough? Turn to page 104

Beating the Casinos at Gambling *for Geniuses*

Flush your money down the toilet.

Yes, that's how easy and fun it is. Let me explain. Over time, both flushing your money down the toilet and gambling will be equally effective at making your money vanish. But since it takes less time to flush your money down the toilet than to gamble it away—and time is money—flushing your money down the toilet is hands-down the winning strategy.

Read enough? Turn to page 104

Flush your money down the toilet.

Yes, that's how easy and fun it is. Let me explain. Over time, both flushing your money down the toilet and gambling will be equally effective at making your money vanish. But since it takes less time to flush your money down the toilet than to gamble it away—and time is money—flushing your money down the toilet is hands-down the winning strategy.

Read enough? Turn to page 104

Yep, that's it. That's the whole book.

We know that gamblers don't seem to learn from repetition, but honestly, how many more times do we need to repeat it? If fifty times is not enough, we suggest you read the book again. As many times as it takes.

You got the point right away? That's wonderful news, but not surprising. After all… you are a Genius!

Beating the Casinos at Gambling *for Geniuses*

 Use it as a notebook to record how much money you made using the technique explained in this book. (The left sided pages have been lined for your convenience.)

 "Gift it forward" Give the book to unsuspecting friends, family members, or colleagues—and help them earn more money gambling—just like you.

 Add it to your *Just for Geniuses*™ collection. No promises, but serious collectors are expecting the value of all *Just for Geniuses*™ branded merchandise to substantially rise in the decades and centuries ahead.

Nonetheless, we would like to thank you for taking the time to read this book.

We couldn't write books like this without readers like you to support us. Any feedback you give would be greatly appreciated. We have fragile egos, so be gentle about it. Or funny.

Please give us feedback at
www.justforgeniuses.com/feedback

Sorry to hear that. But don't despair. The real power of the *Just for Geniuses*™ brand is the flexibility and the ability to customize it **to your needs**. Think gifts, collectibles, promos, charity fund-raising, corporate events, advocacy, and much more.

Depending on your needs, we have the perfect solution for you:

- Submit a customization request to our design team at no cost. (We will try to accommodate everyone's request based on our discretion.)
- Ask our Professional Services team to assist you (minimum order applies.) This is necessary for time-sensitive requests.
- License *Just for Geniuses*™ for your product, service, or media needs. This would give you the most flexibility.

What are you waiting for? Submit your request today at **www.justforgeniuses.com/solutions**

Beating the Casinos at Gambling *for Geniuses*

www.justforgeniuses.com

www.ingramcontent.com/pod-product-compliance
Lightning Source LLC
Chambersburg PA
CBHW070853050426
42453CB00012B/2185